What the Weasel?

an imperfect journal
For battling brain weasels

Find Tori Deaux:

Patreon: http://www.Patreon.com/Qwirks
Facebook: https://www.facebook.com/WeaselsAteMyBrain

Acknowledgements:

A HUGE thank you goes out to Team Qwirk on Patreon; your funding, emotional support and patience make everything possible. To Nicole Fende, Monette Satterfield, Ellie Di Julio and Nikki Lussier? Thank you for all of the pushing, prodding, weasel-poking and hard work you've done over the years. You can't imagine how important your help and contributions have been. And I suppose I should thank my own Brain Weasels for shutting up long enough to get this journal put together!

Credits:

Original art and brain weaselized quotes by Tori Deaux

Book Design by Monette Satterfield

Disclaimer:

The content is not intended to be a substitute for professional advice, diagnosis, or treatment. Always seek the advice of your mental health professional or other qualified health provider with any questions you may have regarding your condition. Ignore any medical advice doled out by brain weasels. They do not know what they're talking about!

Copyright © 2020 Tori Deaux

All rights reserved. This book may not be reproduced in whole, or in part, stored in a retrieval system, or transmitted in any form or by any means – electronic, mechanical, or other – without written permission from the publisher, except by a reviewer, who may quote brief passages in a review. Violators will be fed to the weasels.

Paperback ISBN 978-0-9837659-6-7

Published by Tesseray Publishing LLC,

7635 148th Street West, #329

Apple Valley, MN 55124

www.TesserayPublishing.com

What in the World is a Brain Weasel?

Brain Weasels (weasels for short) are snarling, bitey personifications of the negativity inside of our heads. They're the ghost-memories of red-pen wielding teachers, echoes of that first boyfriend who said we weren't pretty enough, shadows of authority figures who told us we'd never amount to anything. Weasels are our gnawing self-doubts, our inner critics, the bully-hall monitors of our minds... and they are liars.

This journal is a weasel-free space.
You have permission to use it however you like.

- Maybe you'll use it to plan and track your self-care (did you know that weasels hate self-care?)
- Maybe use a page or two and create a record of your successes -- So you got out of bed today? HOORAY! Celebrate by recording that success here.
- You might write down the lies your weasels tell you, then debunk those lies. (I find that bullet points, arrows and underlining makes pointing out the bunk extra enjoyable.)

There are no rules, and if the weasels insist that there are rules, break those rules!

> Start at the back of the journal, or the middle.
> Write and color between lines, or don't.
> Write on the pages upside down.
> Write in the margins, write around and over the illustrations, draw and doodle and scribble right over their weasel faces if that feels good.
> It's totally up to you.

And if the weasels yapp at you about how you're doing it wrong? Tell them to hush!

This is a space for your truths, not theirs.

Happy journaling, Brave Weasel Wrangler!

Toi Deaux

What makes this an "imperfect journal"?

In any creative project, there are imperfections -- those imperfections are the hallmark of human touch. Please expect this journal to be very, um, hallmarked!

Those inevitable embedded mistakes on these pages are a permission slip for your own imperfections. So give your messy handwriting, spelling errors, and hen-scratched doodles free reign; your additions will be perfectly imperfect, and the Weasels don't get to judge you for it.

Why are some of the weasels in costume?

Making brain weasels dress up in goofy costumes takes the sting out of their gnawing, lying ways - it's hard to take a negative thought to heart when we picture it dressed up in pigtails or fairy wings.

And yes, the costumes have meaning:

- The weasels dressed as fairies are tricksters, insisting that they're natural and good and trying to help us. But really, they are just fakes who superglued acorns to their heads.
- The psychic, fortune teller weasels pretend to read other people's minds, making up lies about how everyone feels about us, but they don't know how anyone else feels...it's all lies, lies and damn weasel lies! They also pretend to know the future, predicting disaster no matter what...they're not only fake psychics, they're BAD fake psychics!
- The weasel in pigtails is just a childish mean girl, forever a bully, making a big stink while spritzing perfume and claiming innocence.
- Space weasels remind us that their lies are alien to us, and really "out there."
- The weasels without costumes? Just plain old, garden variety bald-faced naked liars.

And THAT is why the weasels are in costume!

"I've had it with these mother-loving weasels in this mother-loving brain!"
— Not-Quite Samuel L. Jackson

"We are not trying to entertain the weasels. I'll take my chances with the public." — Not-Exactly Walt Disney

"Courage is resistance to weasels, mastery of weasels—not absence of weasels." — Not-Really Mark Twain

"Because it is possible to create—creating one's self, willing to be one's self test—one has weasels." — Not-Quite Rollo May

"You must do the things the weasels say you cannot do." — Something Eleanor Roosevelt didn't say

"If you hear a weasel within you say, 'You cannot paint,' then by all means paint, and the weasel will be silenced."
— Not-Really Vincent Van Gogh

"Our weasels are traitors, and make us lose the good we oft might win, by fearing to attempt." — Not-Quite William Shakespeare

"The worst enemy to creativity is self-doubt. And weasels." — Not-Really Sylvia Plath

"I drank because I wanted to drown my weasels, but now the damn things have learned to swim." — Not what Frida Kahlo said

"The worst loneliness is to not be comfortable with your weasels." — Something Mark Twain didn't write

"I prefer to be true to myself, ... rather than to be false, and to incur my own abhorrence." — Not-Quite Frederick Douglass

"First principle: never to let one's self be beaten down by persons or by events, nor by weasels!" — Not-Exactly Marie Curie

"Humanity needs practical men . . . humanity also needs dreamers. Humanity does not, however, need weasels." — Still not Marie Curie

"People will do anything, no matter how absurd, to avoid facing their own weasels." — Not quite what Carl Jung said

"The first and greatest victory is to conquer your weasels; to be conquered by your weasels is of all things most shameful and vile." — Not exactly what Plato wrote

"Luke, I am your weasel!" — Darth Vader said in an alternate storyline

"The more perfect a person is on the outside, the more weasels they have on the inside." — Sigmund Freud, in another dimension

"Sometimes a weasel is just a weasel."
— Not actually a Sigmund Freud quote

"The greatest weapon against weasels is our ability to choose one thought over another." — Not what William James philosophized

_____
_____
_____
_____
_____
_____
_____
_____
_____
_____
_____
_____
_____
_____
_____
_____
_____
_____

"Knowing your weasels is the beginning of all wisdom." — Not an Aristotle quote

"Suffering is one very long weasel. We cannot divide it by seasons. We can only record its moods, and chronicle its return." — Definitely not Oscar Wilde

"With us, a weasel itself does not progress. It revolves. It seems to circle round one centre of pain." — Still not Oscar Wilde

"I used to think I was the strangest person in the world, with more weasels than anyone." — Not precisely what Frida Kahlo said

"Find out what a person fears most and that is where weasels will develop next." — Not-Really Carl Jung

"He who has overcome his weasels will truly be free." — Not even close to what Aristotle said

"Knowing your weasels is the beginning of all wisdom." — Also not what Aristotle said

"Out, out, damn weasel!"— Maybe Francis Bacon, but certainly not William Shakespeare

"Weaseling out of things is important to learn. It's what separates us from the animals. Except the weasel." — Actually Homer Simpson

"Pain is inevitable; Weasels are optional." — Not a Buddhist proverb

"It is better to conquer your weasels than to win a thousand battles." — Still not the Buddha

Actual Quotes and Attributions

- "I've had it with these mother-#$@!ing snakes in this mother-#$@!ing plane!!" -- Samuel L. Jackson, Snakes On A Plane
- "We are not trying to entertain the critics. I'll take my chances with the public." -- Walt Disney, as quoted in "Disneyland, 1955: Just Take the Santa Ana Freeway to the American Dream" by Karal Ann Marling, in American Art (Winter-Spring 1991)
- "Courage is resistance to fear, mastery of fear - not absence of fear." -- Mark Twain, Pudd'nhead Wilson
- "Because it is possible to create — creating one's self, willing to be one's self, as well as creating in all the innumerable daily activities (and these are two phases of the same process) — one has anxiety. One would have no anxiety if there were no possibility whatever." -- Rollo May, interpreting Søren Kierkegaard in The Meaning of Anxiety
- "You must do the things you think you cannot do" -- Eleanor Roosevelt
- "If you hear a voice within you say 'You cannot paint'... then by all means paint, and that voice will be silenced." -- Van Gogh, Letter to Theo van Gogh Drenthe, 28 October 1883
- "Our doubts are traitors, and make us lose the good we oft might win by fearing to attempt." -- William Shakespeare (Lucio in Measure for Measure Act 1 Scene 4)

- "The worst enemy to creativity is self-doubt." -- Sylvia Plath, The Unabridged Journals of Sylvia Plath
- " I drank because I wanted to drown my sorrows, but now the damn things have learned to swim." -- Frida Kahlo, as quoted in Frida: A Biography of Frida Kahlo by Hayden Herrera
- "The worst loneliness is to not be comfortable with yourself." -- Mark Twain, Huckleberry Finn (?)
- "I prefer to be true to myself, even at the hazard of incurring the ridicule of others, rather than to be false, and to incur my own abhorrence." -- Frederick Douglass Narrative of the Life of Frederick Douglass
- "First principle: never to let one's self be beaten down by persons or by events." -- Marie Curie as quoted in Madame Curie: A Biography by Eve Curie; translated by Vincent Sheean
- "Humanity needs practical men, who get the most out of their work, and, without forgetting the general good, safeguard their own interests. But humanity also needs dreamers, for whom the disinterested development of an enterprise is so captivating that it becomes impossible for them to devote their care to their own material profit... " -- Marie Curie, as quoted in Astrophysics of the Diffuse Universe by Michael A. Dopita and Ralph S. Sutherland
- "People will do anything, no matter how absurd, to avoid facing their own souls" -- Carl Jung, Psychology and Alchemy – Collected Works of C. G. Jung, Volume 12
- "The first and greatest victory is to conquer yourself; to be conquered by yourself is of all things most shameful and vile." -- Plato
- "Luke, I am your Father!" -- Darth Vader

- "The more perfect a person is on the outside, the more demons they have on the inside." -- Sigmund Freud
- "Sometimes a cigar is just a cigar." -- Sigmund Freud
- "The greatest weapon against stress is our ability to choose one thought over another." --William James, American philosopher and psychologist
- "Knowing your self is the beginning of all wisdom." -- Aristotle
- "Suffering is one very long moment. We cannot divide it by seasons. We can only record its moods, and chronicle their return. With us time itself does not progress. It revolves. It seems to circle round one centre of pain." – Oscar Wilde
- "I used to think I was the strangest person in the world, but then I thought there are so many people in the world, there must be someone just like me who feels bizarre and flawed in the same ways I do. " -- Frida Kahlo
- "Find out what a person fears most and that is where he will develop next." -- Carl Jung
- "He who has overcome his fears will truly be free." -- Aristotle
- "Knowing yourself is the beginning of all wisdom." -- Aristotle
- "Out, out, damn spot!" -- William Shakespeare
- "Suffering is one very long moment. We cannot divide it by seasons. We can only record its moods, and chronicle their return." -- Oscar Wilde
- "Weaseling out of things is important to learn. It's what separates us from the animals." -- Matt Groening
- "Pain is certain, suffering is optional." -- Buddha

- "It is better to conquer yourself than to win a thousand battles. Then the victory is yours. It cannot be taken from you, not by angels or by demons, heaven or hell." -- Buddha

www.ingramcontent.com/pod-product-compliance
Lightning Source LLC
Chambersburg PA
CBHW051959290426
44110CB00015B/2308